PORTRAIT of an AGE

SELECTED BY Han de Vries and Peter Hunter-Salomon

BIOGRAPHY AND NOTES BY Peter Hunter-Salomon

PHOTOGRAPHIC LAYOUT BY Han de Vries

TRANSLATED BY Sheila Tobias

Erich Salomon

PORTRAIT
of an AGE

THE MACMILLAN COMPANY, NEW YORK

COLLIER-MACMILLAN LIMITED, LONDON

Copyright © Collier-Macmillan Canada, Ltd., 1967
Originally published in German, under the title
Porträt einer Epoche, © 1963 by Verlag Ullstein GmbH,
Frankfurt/M — Berlin

Library of Congress Catalog Card Number: 66-29845

The Macmillan Company, New York
Collier-Macmillan Canada Ltd., Toronto, Ontario
PRINTED IN FRANCE

Briand called him "the king of the indiscreet." Another statesman of the time admitted, "One can hold conferences these days without ministers but not without Dr. Salomon." He was known on two continents for his skill at penetrating the best-guarded political meetings and for his pictures of places which no photographer heretofore had dared to shoot. *Graphic,* the London magazine, coined the phrase "candid camera" for his work. Salomon came from a well-to-do Berlin banking family, but when the family lost its fortune, he had to begin again from scratch. Along with millions of other Jews, Salomon met death at the hands of the Nazis.

Contents

Who Was Erich Salomon?

by Peter Hunter-Salomon

Until I was fourteen years old I thought my father was a burglar. He was an amateur builder, with a huge closet filled with remarkable gadgets, all of which looked to me like burglary tools. Besides, he rarely came home before one A.M.

I cherished my fantasy until one night, returning home, my father found me asleep behind a door. I had planned to spy on him. But he had, as it turned out, just returned from Ullstein, the most respectable publishers. I was forced to confess what I had suspected, and, of course, he was royally amused.

In 1938, six years before his death, I saw my father for the last time in London, where I had fled from the Nazis. Because the memory of a son may have grown inexact in the twenty-eight years that have since passed, it would perhaps be wise to call upon others to fill in the picture of Erich Salomon.

Tom Hopkinson, former editor of *Picture Post,* described him thus: "In appearance, he was a man of medium height. He was possessed of considerable dignity, and had a rather surprising aura of white hair which used to run up into two big tufts. That was the reason Briand gave him the name of *l'homme à la tête Mephistophèle.* When agitated, he used to brush these up, and look more demoniacal than ever."

Another friend, M. Neven du Mont, wrote of him: "He was one of the quietest, gentlest and most endearing men I have met. There was a modesty about him which is the hall-mark of greatness. At the same time, he had a subtle sense of humour, which shone through his seriousness like soft sunshine on a day in mid-winter. He was a most unobtrusive person, a man who never raised his voice or boasted or pushed himself

forward. He had the air of a thinker and philosopher. He was full of tolerance and understanding, and these qualities no doubt gave him such a deep insight into his fellow men. Salomon, I feel certain, never consciously hurt or harmed anyone in his life."

I first became acquainted with my father when he returned home after World War I and four years in a French prisoner-of-war camp. As a prisoner he had made himself camp leader and as an interpreter had refreshed his knowledge of French. I was five. At first I suffered some shyness in his presence. I hated to be picked up by strangers and swung through the air, for example. And that was how he greeted me then— his "big" boy.

My father was born in the year 1886 to the family of Emil Salomon, banker, the fourth of five children. My grandfather Emil was a member of the Berlin stock exchange, and his family took an active part in the artistic and intellectual life of the city. My grandmother belonged to the Sonnemann clan, founders of the *Frankfurter Zeitung.*

In the aftermath of the 1914-18 war the family's fortunes had melted away to such an extent that my father had to go out and earn some money. After having tried vainly to find an opening on the stock exchange, he started a rental agency for electric cars (gas was rationed) and motorcycles with sidecars "with chauffeur." For the cars there were drivers he could hire. But for the motorcycle he was sole chauffeur himself; he advertised his services in the following way:

A doctor of law will drive you in a sidecar while he gives you valuable information as to how the German mark's devaluation is related to the price of gold.

When gasoline flowed freely again the car rental business hit hard times. Salomon became a partner in the Duysen piano factory. But despite his tireless efforts and his enthusiasm, the instruments built by the renowned firm remained in their warehouses. The company went into bankruptcy.

Salomon had to find other work. Someone sent him to the Ullstein publishing people because they had the reputation of taking on and encouraging young people with good ideas. He was assigned to the publicity department, a group of ambitious and talented young men, some of whom later played a significant role in American publishing. One of his duties was to arrange for the construction of enormous iron billboards flanking all the railroad tracks, onto which giant posters advertising the magazine *Uhu* were pasted. The job led in the course of time to countless court actions involving farmers who did not want to fulfill the obligations they had assumed by contract. For one of these cases Salomon needed some photographs in order to bring home a point to the court—pictures he took with an unwieldy camera borrowed from Ullstein. He became interested in the new art, and almost at the same time, again by accident, his interest was rewarded.

One day, while sitting in a small restaurant near the Spree, a sudden, heavy rainstorm began to wreak havoc in the neighborhood. A passing newsboy called out, "Have you heard that some of the trees uprooted by the storm skidded onto some beach lockers and that a woman has been killed?" The journalist in Salomon was born. He took off like a shot for the nearest photographer. Some of the pictures taken that day were bought by the Ullstein papers. Salomon received 100 marks for them and paid the photographer 90 as a fee. The next day he went into a camera store and asked to see a camera for himself: the Ermanox.

This relatively small camera used 4.5 by 6 cm. plates and had an *f*.2 lens. As early as 1926 the camera had been advertised with the slogan "What you see you can photograph," but hardly anyone had responded to the campaign.

Salomon's first shots were made outdoors and were generally overexposed. I can remember clearly one excursion we made into the Grunewald. Salomon kept taking and retaking bad pictures. The camera had hardly any depth of focus, and if the distance was not set exactly the shots were blurred. But Salomon mastered these technical difficulties and experimented with indoor pictures, which were almost impossible to overexpose.

One day, just as he began to show successful results at Ullstein, someone mentioned that there was a sensational trial—the Hein trial—taking place at Coburg, about 400 kilometers from Berlin. Salomon jumped into a taxi and persuaded the driver to drive him there. He returned from Coburg with pictures which created a sensation. Never before had anyone been able to capture the atmosphere of a trial so perfectly with a camera. (Why his camera had not been confiscated in the courtroom, where it was illegal to take pictures, no one could figure out at the time. "No one took any notice of me," he explained later. "Don't you remember that I took a hat with me? I cut a hole in the crown and hid the camera in the hat. When they realized what was happening they wanted to confiscate my negatives. But I remembered that old lizard's trick—putting what is useless into the mouth of the enemy—and gave them only a few unexposed plates.")

With one day's work Salomon had now earned two months' pay. His superiors seemed to be impressed with this new kind of journalism, and they made no difficulties when he decided to quit his regular job for free-lancing.

Three years later, in 1931, Salomon decided to celebrate his forty-fifth birthday in a manner befitting his reputation as the first "candid camera" man. He invited almost 400 members of Berlin society to the Hotel Kaiserhof—ministers, ambassadors, and their wives—and then astounded his guests by showing them pictures he had clandestinely taken of them at numerous conferences and parties. Everyone admired the photographs, and the evening was a great success. But Salomon's popularity in Berlin society proved to be short-lived. One year later, a man whose name would become all too famous chose the same hotel as the jumping-off station for his next goal: the Reichs Chancellery. When Adolf Hitler came onto the scene Salomon was no longer welcome at the Kaiserhof.

In his book *Famous Contemporaries in Unguarded Moments*—which appeared in 1931—Salomon gives an amusing résumé of his work —in this case, picture-taking at the Reichstag. Even the chapter headings are significant. They all begin with the word "fight."

1. The fight for the possibility of a photograph —for permission to set up in a particular place; for permission to photograph; fighting the prejudice and fear of flash bulbs (which Salomon never used).

2. The fight for the photograph itself—fights with employees, with door guards, with self-appointed interferers; fighting bad lighting, thick cigar smoke, over-rapid movement, and so on.

3. The fight after the photograph has been taken—for the publication of the picture; fighting editorial deadlines; fighting objections by editors (for example, the picture editor of a London Sunday paper: "Toscanini I don't know. What I need are football pictures.").

Then Salomon adds up his experiences and identifies "the power of the *fait accompli*." "If you stand before the doors of the meeting room and ask the man in charge to let you in, it is not hard for that man to tell you all the reasons he can't let you in. If, however, before the meeting begins, you are already in the room, the man in charge has to ask you to leave that room—and this requires a far greater psychological effort on his part.

"The power of the principle of *fait accompli* is even greater when it takes place at that precise moment when, according to all human calcula-

tions, it is no longer possible to cancel it out. I used this experience once with great success.... The newly formed cabinet of Hermann Müller was supposed to present itself to the Reichstag, and it was very important that I get a good picture of the new Chancellor during his opening speech. With this in mind I went to see President Löbe and asked him to save me a place on the Reichsrat dais just once for this important event. The President was not unwilling to help, but he thought that at an opening speech the entire Reichsrat dais would be full and that men would in fact stand up to listen, keeping me from having a clear view. This made sense to me. Therefore I asked one of the Reichstag ushers whether any of the deputies was sick or on vacation, anyone whose place I might take. 'That is really very simple, Herr Doktor,' the man said; 'the Chancellor's seat itself is vacant.' Obviously that spot was perfect, above all because the seat was precisely the right distance—four and a half meters—from the lectern. But I had the feeling I would be peremptorily thrown out if I appeared in that particular seat before the session began. I had to dream up a stratagem.

"I waited until President Löbe had given Chancellor Müller the floor, figuring that no one would interrupt the Chancellor just to chase me out of his seat. Besides, in the event the Chancellor noticed me at all, he was not likely to break his train of thought to take care of something for which he was not responsible anyway. The only danger remaining came from the deputies seated around me. I armed myself against this contingency. After the Chancellor had said a few words I started moving toward his vacated seat. I looked neither to the left nor to the right. This was vital if I was not to risk losing the peace and quiet indispensable to photographing under pressure.

"I had hardly sat down when Representative Dittmann, seated diagonally across from me, turned to me and, thinking that I was a newly elected deputy, said: 'But you're no Social Democrat. You can't sit here.' I whispered that I only intended to stay a few moments and handed him a picture in which he himself was clearly recognizable. As I had expected, he became so lost in this picture that I was able to take my photographs. Leaving my seat would have been disturbing, and because no one else seemed to mind my presence I remained seated until the Chancellor's speech came to an end. Meantime I photographed members of the Reichsrat as they listened.

"When I met President Löbe in the corridor after the session he said: 'But Herr Doktor, we never agreed to that. Never before in the history of the Reichstag has a layman sat among the deputies.' "

M. Neven-du Mont tells a similar and equally charming story about a joint visit to the Reichstag made with Salomon.

"I once visited Salomon in Berlin, and together we went to the Reichstag. He confided to me that he had figured out a way to take photographs during the session, something hitherto strictly forbidden. Suddenly he slipped wordlessly from my side in the direction of the speaker. But as soon as he pulled out his camera a uniformed guard appeared, grabbed him by the arm, and took him away.

"I was curious to see what would happen next. The guard demanded Salomon's pass. Because Salomon did not have one, he turned and moved slowly on, the guard following him. But because with every step Salomon went a little faster, their little march developed into a real—if silent— chase up and down the aisles of the Reichstag. I saw Salomon turn suddenly around, raise his camera, and snap a picture of his pursuer.

"Then he said quietly: 'If you do not leave me alone, I'll report you. I already have your picture.' The simple threat worked. The guard apologized and begged Salomon to forget the whole incident —the typical Prussian reaction."

In 1929 Salomon took his camera to England. Again I quote him: "For the English the notion that someone would be photographing anywhere without having previously asked permission is so absurd that they assume every time that permission has been granted.

"I found this out first at the annual banquet of the Royal Academy, the most exclusive occasion of the London season. A newspaper called me on the telephone on Saturday at one P.M. and asked me to take photographs of the banquet. I suggested right away that they assign an Englishman, as assistant, to point out the prominent guests to me, because I had then been in London only a short time. They said, however, that that would not be necessary because 'at this dinner everyone is important.' I agreed finally to try to do it alone and asked them to send me an invitation. Then they admitted they didn't have an invitation for me, but were certain that I would be able to 'organize' one. I considered negotiating with the Secretary of the Academy, a total waste of time. On top of that no one in London can be reached on a Saturday afternoon anyway. So I waited until evening, put on my tuxedo, and went to the banquet where—following my basic rule—I arrived exactly one hour late.

"This one-hour rule is based on the observation that if one comes too late, doormen and the like are already tired out from the battle and in better humor. It happened as expected. No one asked for my invitation. Someone took my overcoat, gave me a ticket, and I climbed the stairs and came out on the floor above, directly vis-à-vis an easel which displayed the seating plan.

"I studied this card intently and finally discovered one name I recognized, the Home Secretary's. I decided to try the legal way first and entered the banquet room packed with five hundred important people. I succeeded in reaching the Minister unmolested, bade him good day, and asked for his help. He had some reservations, but he was willing enough to ask the opinion of an aged member of the Academy who sat next to him. This man's answer matched his face, and the Minister turned to me rather upset and said: 'He says that it is quite impossible, that it has never been done before.' . . . After I had already taken at least twelve different pictures a gentleman came up to me and asked what I, in fact, was doing. I told him I was photographing. 'Yes, but for whom are you taking these photographs?' he asked. I wasn't prepared for this question and to say something answered, 'For the weekly *Graphic!*' 'But they haven't asked permission!'—to which I answered with exaggerated surprise, 'Oh, haven't they?' My interrogator left me alone for a while but then turned back and said, 'The Secretary of the Academy says that this has never been done before.' 'That is just why I am doing it,' I rejoined with the most disarming, innocuous smile I could muster. The gentleman apparently could not deal with this logic, so he left me for a second time. After a while he returned again and said, 'Are you Dr. Erich Salomon?' I had taken shots the day before at the preview of this art exhibition, and that morning one of my photographs had appeared with my name under it in the *Daily Mirror.* I did not deny who I was, whereupon the gentleman told me the secretary was not averse to my photographing as much as I wished so long as I did not ask anyone to pose for me. I said laughing, 'That's what I never do.' But at this very moment Prince George, the King's fourth son, entered the hall accompanied by the President of the Academy, and both men planted themselves in precisely the right place in front of my camera. I gave my interviewer a meaningful glance. He made a quick turn and left my victims to me."

Once Salomon found himself in a highly unpleasant situation, which he describes in the following manner: "In 1931 there was an important secret conference between the German and the French which was, in fact, held on the balcony of the Parisian Ministry of the Interior. I had hidden myself in a neighboring room and had already taken some photographs of the German delegates through a window which opened onto the balcony. Suddenly the French delegation walked by on their way to the balcony, and I heard M. Briand murmur: *'Ah! Le terrible docteur.'* This was the second nickname by which he knew me. M. Tardieu had introduced me to him in The Hague with the words, 'Here is M. Salomon, the king of the indiscreet.' Somewhat encouraged by M. Briand's remark, I followed the French ministers onto the balcony, where I took a whole series of pictures. As I was about to use my last plate, M. François-Poncet—then *chef de cabinet* to M. Laval—suddenly got up behind me and said: 'I do not think you are permitted to take even a single photograph. Therefore may I suggest that you sit down. Perhaps you have some good ideas that could help us solve this problem.' The other statesmen, who until then had paid me no attention at all, now interrupted their conversation and turned to me. Had I then taken a photograph, there would have been nothing artless and natural about the expressions on their faces. After a few moments, which to me seemed an eternity, the diplomats relaxed their stony expressions, but the icy silence lasted until M. Laval began again to speak. Only then did I shoot my last picture."

In 1935 King George V and Queen Mary celebrated their silver anniversary. Salomon felt that in London itself there was little prospect of interesting photographs, so he drove to Windsor Castle. The magnificent buildings enchanted him, and he got the idea of photographing the Castle at night with a special illumination of his own design. He loaded the old Rolls-Royce, which he usually used to drive around London, with twelve auto batteries. These were then connected in series to provide electric current for a few powerful light reflectors. Thus equipped, he drove happily around the Castle grounds for eight nights. One night a policeman stopped him and asked what he was doing. "I am waiting for the moon," answered Salomon. The policeman reflected for a bit and then asked: "Have you an appointment?"

Once I found a letter in which my father mentioned how he had hunted up a pair of iron spikes, the kind used to climb telegraph poles. He added them to a collection which among other things included a pair of old field telephones he had once planned to use if he ever had to take photographs from the roof of a moving furniture truck while needing to stay in contact with the driver. The telephones had never been employed, because the chairman of the conference in question heard of his plan to take candid photographs and promptly sent him an official invitation. But the telephones are also associated with an amusing story. Salomon once found himself in Switzerland on his way to France when a zealous customs official came upon one of them. "What is that, Monsieur?" "That is my telephone." "Ah, so. Certainly, Monsieur." The man respectfully touched the peak of his cap. With a high-placed personage who carried his own telephone around with him one didn't wish to take chances.

Among Salomon's "equipment" was also a cleverly fabricated "hearing device" fitted out with earphones and a large black cloth sling ostensibly designed for a broken arm. It was with the help of that "sling" that Salomon was able to get the only photograph in existence of the United States Supreme Court in session. There were also a few "diplomatic pouches" with built-in hiding places for an Ermanox.

Salomon regarded himself as an historian. At those functions that he did not succeed in getting admitted to, despite all efforts and preparations, he either shot his pictures through the window or worked out more or less "symbolic" photographs—for example, the dozing coat checker guarding the ministers' hats in the middle of the night. Such tricks, which Salomon was using for the first time, are now standard photo-journalistic practice.

In 1933, after Hitler had come to power, my family moved to Holland because the parents of my mother, who had been born in Rotterdam, were able to give us temporary shelter. In 1943 my parents, together with my brother Dirk, who was then twenty-three years old, were deported, and in 1944 all of them died in the gas chambers of Auschwitz.

My father's legacy lies in his work and in the legends which grew up around him. There is a Salomon legend—it is not always accurate but it is always characteristic.

For example, it is true that he once made use of a window washer's ladder in order to photograph a Hague conference through the window. However, it is only a myth that a minister's secretary pushed him off that ladder. It is also true that he once hid his camera in three thick, hollowed-out mathematics books in order to photograph a roulette game in Monte Carlo. I am dubious, however, about the story which has it that he kneeled once for thirty minutes in simulated prayer beside the bier of a cardinal, his camera hidden in a Bible.

Although a number of famous photographers have been influenced by Salomon, I wish to mention only one by name: Henri Cartier-Bresson, who has discovered and shown to us human life in all its fullness and variety.

"Salomon and Cartier-Bresson," writes Norman Hall, publisher of the British photo magazine *Photography,* "perceive human life and portray it impartially and almost impersonally. Their cameras see and report everything; they are unprejudiced and incorruptible."

It was precisely prejudice that kept Salomon from the Hotel Kaiserhof once Hitler had worked himself in. It was the same prejudice from which he died. As a liberal and a man drawn to his fellow men, Salomon was incapable of recognizing the danger for himself in the bestial Nazi regime. Therefore what remains is only his work, in which one can discern the ideals of a talented and civilized European.

PORTRAIT of an AGE

CHAPTER ONE

The Epoch of the League of Nations

The League of Nations is a human creation, a synthesis of the ideal and the real. But whoever criticizes the League of Nations or finds fault with the slow progress it makes dare not deprive the League of his cooperation. He dare not run the risk that all those nightmares, all that blood and violence, might come again to pass.

—GUSTAV STRESEMANN

A summit meeting in 1928: The architects of Franco-German rapprochement, Aristide Briand and Dr. Gustav Stresemann, meet in the Hotel Splendide in Lugano with the British Foreign Minister, Sir Austen Chamberlain. From left to right: Zaleski, Poland; Adatci, Japan; Chamberlain; Stresemann; Briand; Scialoia, Italy.

At the Quai d'Orsay in Paris on August 27, 1928: The signing of the Kellogg-Briand Pact, which by formally prohibiting war was supposed to lessen international tensions. Fifteen nations agreed to condemn aggressive war; other nations later joined the pact. This photograph is the view from the seat of a Polish diplomat who had not come. It shows the front row with, as guests of honor, from right to left, French Minister of War Paul Painlevé; the American Ambassador to Paris, Myron Herrick; Mme. Hymans, the wife of the Belgian Foreign Minister; the President of France, Raymond Poincaré; President of the French Senate, Paul Doumer, and Mme. Doumer; farther along, Edouard Herriot (with dark hair).

Fritjof Nansen being interviewed by Miss Round, a British journalist. The Norwegian scientist was famed for the Arctic explorations made with the *Fram,* the first ship whose hull was designed to withstand the pressure of ice. In 1922 he was awarded the Nobel Peace Prize for saving refugees of many nationalities. Even today he is remembered by the phrase "Nansen passport." This photograph was made in September, 1928, in the entrance hall of the Palace of the League of Nations in Geneva and is one of the last taken before Nansen's death in 1930.

Glimpses of the League of Nations at work in 1928. The above picture shows the French labor-union leader Léon Jouhaux. Right, Miss Vacarescu, Rumanian poetess and deputy to the League of Nations, eloquently pleading the cause of peace.

9

◄ Two listeners in the press box during a long-winded speech by Mr. Voldemaras, Premier of Lithuania.

An incident on the sidelines: Albert Thomas, the tireless director of the International Labor Organization, still known as the I.L.O., requests an additional secretary for his office. He signs the request before giving it to a friend. He impatiently awaits the results, and in the last picture his secretary Viple informs him of the affirmative answer.

15

The French weekly *Vu* called this photograph "Conversation Animée." French delegate S. Grumbach, German delegate Rudolf Breitscheid, and French delegate Joseph Paul-Boncour confer after a strenuous session, in the lobby of the League of Nations Palace, September, 1928. Britscheid, a Social-Democrat, died in Buchenwald concentration camp in 1944.

The Japanese delegate, Baron Adatci, considered one of the most intelligent delegates at the League of Nations. He never missed a session. In 1929 his tact and abilities decisively influenced the war-reparations conference at The Hague. Later he became president of the Permanent Court of International Justice at The Hague, and, after three years there, he died in Amsterdam in 1939.

The photograph above shows Adatci at a meeting of the League of Nations in September, 1929; he is seen on the right during a committee meeting with the British delegate, Lord Cushendun.

Politics at lunch in Geneva in September, 1928. Lord Cushendun had invited Briand (with his ever-present cigarette), Hermann Müller, the Social-Democratic Chancellor of Germany, Adatci, and others to the terrace of the Hotel d'Angleterre. Next to Müller (in the middle, in front of the waiter) is the Italian Foreign Minister, Vittorio Scialoia (facing the camera), and Baron Karl von Schubert (with his back to the camera), State Secretary of the German Foreign Office.

◄ Aristide Briand in the *Salle des Pas Perdus,* the lobby of the League of Nations Palace. This photograph pleased Briand so much that he ordered six prints of it.

Briand leaves a Geneva Conference, hesitant as to how much he should tell the press. ►

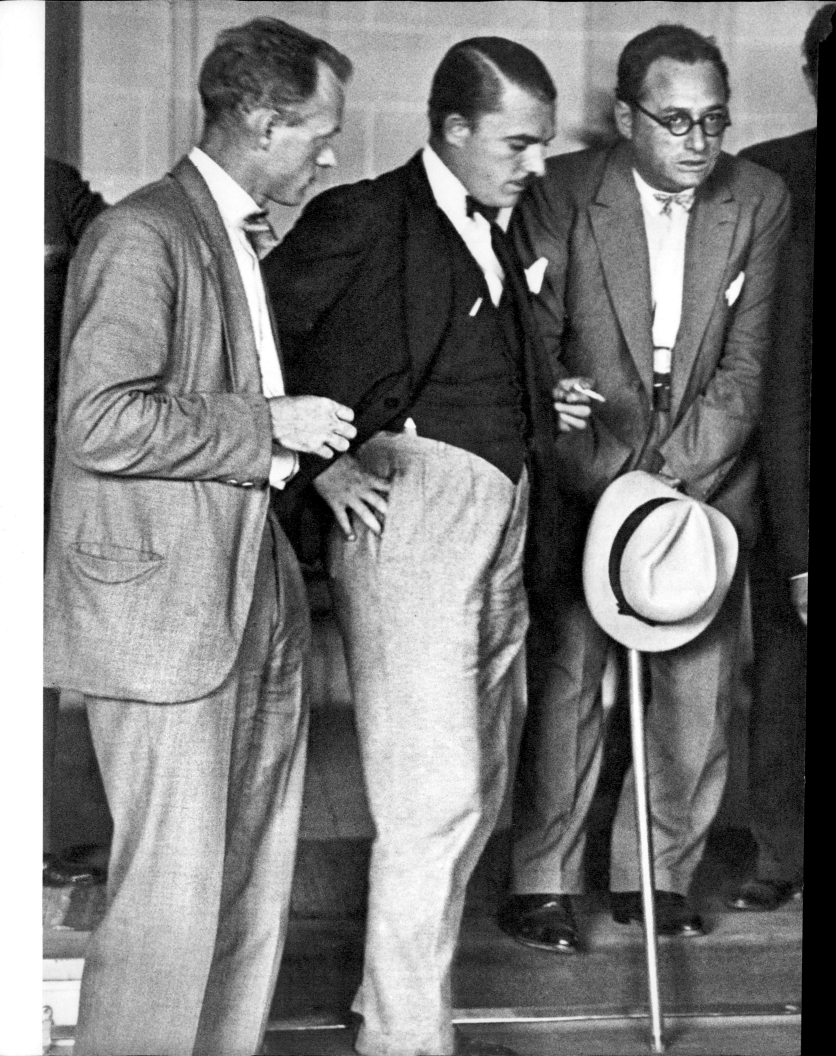

23

CHAPTER TWO

Germany in 1930

The Weimar Republic failed to develop a "governing class." The middle classes, themselves in awe of authority, had never forgiven the republic for the defeat of 1918; the working classes, with no social revolution to inspire them, were loyal, devoted, but ineffective. The economic crisis of 1929–33 did not give the deathblow to the republic; at most it drew attention to the fact that the republic was dead. Any system can stand in fair weather; it is tested when the storm begins to blow. This test the German republic could not pass; with few supporters and no roots, it fell at the first rumble of thunder.

—A. J. P. TAYLOR

Cabinet meeting of the German Government in 1929. From left to right: Dr. Josef Wirth; State Secretary Dr. Hermann Pünder; Social-Democratic Chancellor Hermann Müller; Dr. Hjalmar Schacht, President of the Reichsbank.

Cabinet crisis of Müller's government. After the resignation of Finance Minister Hilferding in December, 1929, Chancellor Müller confers with State Secretaries Dr. Hermann Pünder (left) and Dr. Otto Meissner (right) in the Zeppelin room of the Reichstag.

At the banquet in honor of the historian Hans Delbrück on the occasion of his eightieth birthday. The upper picture shows ▶
Dr. Otto Gessler, former German Minister of Defense, telling a joke to Dr. Carl Petersen, Mayor of Hamburg. Professor Ernst
Jäckh, Director of the Berlin *Hochschule für Politik* (left), and Schacht try to listen. In the lower picture Gessler is now telling
Schacht the same joke while Petersen waits for the reaction. Some time later, on the occasion of the resignation of Schacht as
President of the Reichsbank, Salomon had a less friendly encounter with him. Schacht walked toward him, stared at him through
the view finder mounted on the camera, and snarled, "If you take a photograph here, Doctor, I'll break your camera."

A banker and two socialists: Franz von Mendelssohn, President of the International Chamber of Commerce (left), with Prussian Prime Minister Otto Braun and Chancellor Hermann Müller.

Two female politicians of 1930: Katharina von Kardorff-Oheimb, wife of a Reichstag deputy, and Ada Schmidt-Beil.

In 1930 King Fuad of Egypt
visited Berlin, and President von
Hindenburg gave a reception in
his honor. Because photographs
were not permitted, this picture
was shot from the bathroom window of State Secretary Meissner's
apartment. Hindenburg himself
can be recognized in the second
window from the left.

The Egyptian Ambassador in Berlin, Afifi Pasha (right), also gave a reception for King Fuad, who is seen at the left of the picture together with the Apostolic Nuncio in Berlin, Cardinal Pacelli, later Pope Pius XII.

Gala performance at the Berlin State Opera. Next to the King and Hindenburg are Paul Löbe (left), President of the Reichstag, and Frau Löbe (right).

Gustav Stresemann at a meeting of the
League of Nations on the occasion of
his last speech to that body (September 9, 1929). He died on October 3
of the same year.

Stresemann with journalists in a Geneva café.

The sea resort Scheveningen near The Hague, in Holland. This is where most of the delegates lived during the conferences of 1929 and 1930. On the terrace of the Hotel Kurhaus (note distinctive cupola in picture on left) are Stresemann and his biographer Henry Bernhard, together in the left of the picture below.

During the first Hague Reparations Conference Philip Snowden (later Lord Snowden) played a key role. Here he is seen first as speaker, then thoughtfully puffing a cigarette during a press luncheon. Next to him sit Belgian Foreign Minister Paul Hymans and German Foreign Minister Dr. Julius Curtius. Far left is Austrian Chancellor Johann Schober.

Drowsing under the hats of the ministers, the hat checker patiently awaits the end of a late session in the Anjema Restaurant. ▶

41

At midnight the discussion in the conference room at the Anjema Restaurant was still going strong—at 1 A.M. it is flagging. The photograph above shows, from left to right, Professor Hesnard, the French interpreter; Moldenhauer, the German Finance Minister (with his back to the camera); Tardieu, the French Premier; Curtius, the German Foreign Minister; and Chéron, the French Finance Minister.

◀ German Reichstag Deputy Eisenberger, Chairman of the Bavarian Bauernpartei (Farmers' Party), overcome by exhaustion. When this photograph, taken in the Reichstag, was published in 1930, Eisenberger's party protested and demanded that the chairmen of the other parties ought also to be photographed asleep.

At a private session of the Reichstag in 1930 the English pacifist Lord Cecil of Chelwood gave a lecture. Among the listeners, from left to right: Albert Einstein; von Guérard, the German Minister of Transportation; Professor Bredt, the German Minister of Justice; and General von Seeckt.

Von Seeckt, who more than anyone else had contributed to the rebirth of the German Army, seen during lunch in the restaurant of the Reichstag. According to the Treaty of Versailles, the German Army was to be limited to 100,000 men. It was von Seeckt who invented the scheme of training these for no longer than three months, then taking in a new batch of recruits. Thus, in the 1930s, the German Army was much more powerful than the Allies had expected.

The Communist deputy Ernst Torgler at lunch with members of his party in the restaurant of the Reichstag.

Dr. Heinrich Brüning, German Chancellor from 1930-32, vainly attempted to contain the economic crisis by means of a series of ▶ emergency measures, the well-remembered *Notverordnungen*. He is seen here introducing his budget in February, 1931.

The oldest deputy of the Reichstag, Klara Zetkin, famous Communist and feminist, with a visitor in the parliamentary lobby.

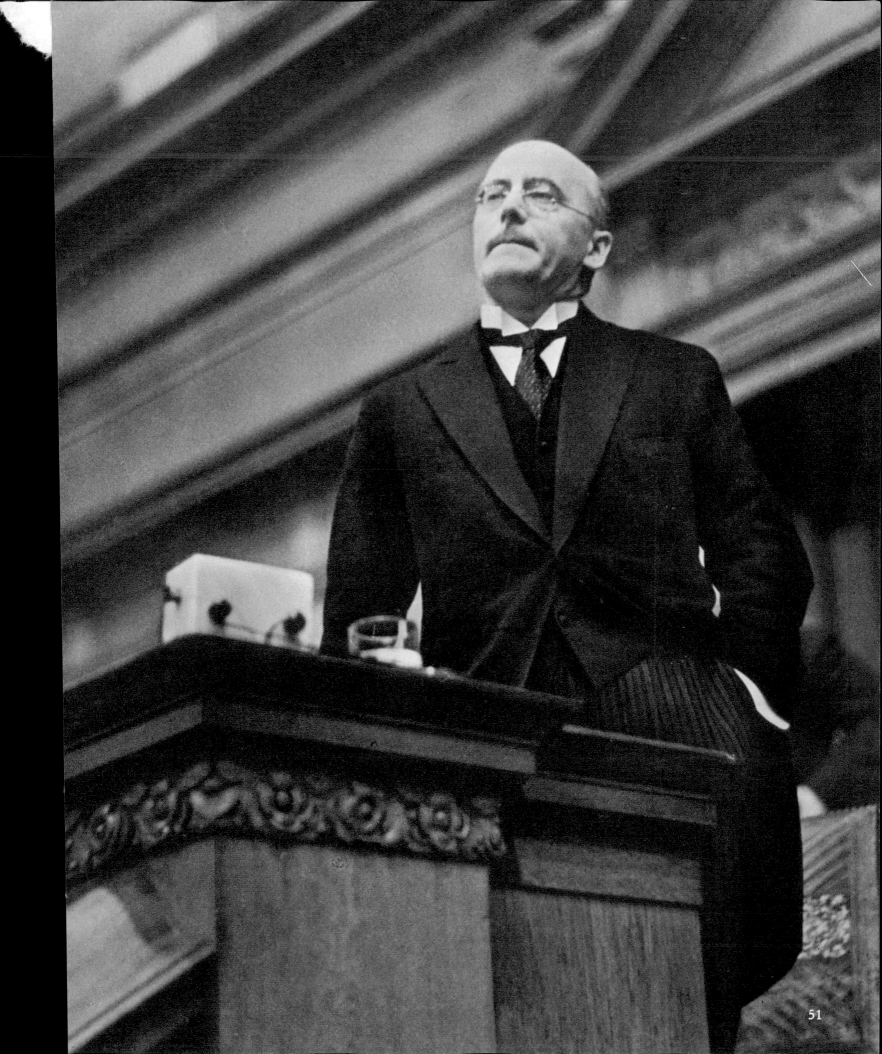

The visitors' gallery in the Reichstag (above). Right, the Brüning cabinet in the Reichstag seen from the stenographer's seat. From left: Schiele, Minister of Food; Schätzel, Minister of the Post; Dr. Wirth, Minister of the Interior; Dr. Curtius, Foreign Minister; Groener, Minister of Defense; Dr. Dietrich, Finance Minister and Vice-Chancellor.

Two years before Hitler's take-over the National Socialists were the second largest party in the Reichstag. This picture shows one section of Nazi deputies seated with their backs to the President during an attempt to disturb the session.

The National Socialist deputies at this point have walked out of the session, only Dr. Joseph Goebbels (standing) remaining as an observer. After a while, dressed in brown shirts, the Nazis return to their places (next page). This was, of course, in flagrant contravention of the rule prohibiting the wearing of uniforms by deputies when in session.

Dr. Hans Luther, President of the ▶
Reichsbank, in conversation with Chancellor Heinrich Brüning.

On a hot August day in 1930 the Brüning cabinet held a session in the garden of the Chancellor's palace. From left to right: Dr. Wachsmann, Ministerial Director of the Finance Ministry; Dr. Schiele, Minister of Food; Dr. Wirth, Minister of the Interior; Dr. Dietrich, Vice-Chancellor and Finance Minister; Chancellor Brüning; Dr. Pünder, State Secretary of the Chancellery. Across from Dr. Dietrich is Prussian Minister of Welfare Hirtsiefer.

CHAPTER THREE

Europe and Its Conferences

France had witnessed many experiments. She had seen the Socialist Snowden in England fail with the policy of "wait and see" to solve the economic problem, and with his financial reforms to reduce the public expenditure. She had witnessed the Conservative Hoover in the United States fail in his attempt to exorcise the evil with injections of credit. She had seen Brüning in Germany fail in his effort to reduce cost prices below sale prices. From all these tragic mishaps the rulers of France were to draw no lesson.

—Paul Reynaud

British diplomatic figures during a reception in Berlin in August, 1931. From left to right: Max Planck; Prime Minister Ramsay MacDonald of England; Albert Einstein; Dr. Dietrich, German Finance Minister; Mr. Schmitz, of I. G. Farben; and Dr. Curtius, German Foreign Minister.

In September, 1931, for the first time since World War I, French statesmen came to Germany. Briand and Laval visited Berlin. At a reception in the Chancellor's Palace no photographers were permitted to be present; this photograph could only be taken through the curtained window. From right to left: Dr. Brüning; Briand; Philippe Berthelot, Permanent Undersecretary to the French Foreign Ministry; Fernand Léger, Briand's *chef de cabinet*.

In July, 1931, Brüning and Curtius visited Paris. At a banquet in their honor held at the Quai d'Orsay Briand learned from his chief of protocol that press photographers had not been allowed in. Briand doubted this and wagered that at least one would be there. Slowly he peered around the room. When he finally discovered Salomon he called out, "Ah, le voilà! Le roi des indiscrets." Left, next to Briand, is Paul Reynaud, Minister of Colonial Affairs; to the right, Champetier de Rives, Minister of Pensions; Edouard Herriot; and Léon Bérard, Minister of Justice.

◄ In August, 1931, Brüning and Curtius also visited Rome. At a tea reception in the gardens of the Villa d'Este the Chief of the Security Guard (in white uniform) hovered about Mussolini. Left, behind the Duce, is Associated Press correspondent Louis P. Lochner.

Evening party in the Hotel Excelsior in Rome. At the table from left to right: Mussolini, Dr. Brüning, Dr. Curtius, and the Italian Foreign Minister Dino Grandi. Five detectives tried to stop the photographer.

In July, 1931, the German and French delegations to the Seven-Power Conference in London traveled together in a special train made available by the French Government for the Paris-London trip. In the parlor car from left to right: Philippe Berthelot, Permanent Undersecretary to the French Foreign Ministry; Chancellor Brüning; Paul Hymans, Belgian Foreign Minister; Dr. Curtius, German Foreign Minister; Briand, French Foreign Minister; Premier Laval; and André François-Poncet, Laval's cabinet chief.

In front of the Foreign Office in London, official cars wait for the delegates to the Seven-Power Conference on the German ▶ financial crisis. Ramsay MacDonald accompanies Briand to his car.

73

At the end of August, 1931, the economic crisis in England necessitated the formation of a coalition government. On August ▶
26th the new government gave its first press conference in the Locarno Room of the Foreign Office. Stanley Baldwin (left), Lord
President of the Council, and Prime Minister Ramsay MacDonald make some effort to understand questions put in broken
English. An English journalist called this shot a photographic cartoon: "Our government—not only old, but deaf."

David Lloyd George at his desk in the year 1929. This is one of the very rare posed photographs by Salomon. On the table is an
issue of the magazine *Graphic,* whose photo editor coined the phrase "candid camera" for Salomon's photographs.

Prime Minister Ramsay MacDonald on a Sunday stroll, followed by two detectives (next page).

CHAPTER FOUR

The Year in Geneva

Today a hero is no longer visible. We avoid the word. World-shaking decisions do not lie in the hands of an individual who can grasp them and, for some span of time, keep them to himself. Decision is absolute only in the realm of the personal fate of an individual. It appears almost always relative in terms of the giant apparatuses which govern our present. It is only because the mass-soul needs to feel admiration that it creates heroes for itself. Whether these heroes are honored for their virtuosity, their daring, or their political fame, an individual can be pushed into the center of the public eye only for a single moment. In a little while he is entirely forgotten and the spotlight moves on to shine on another.

—KARL JASPERS

The Hotel Beau Rivage in Lausanne, headquarters of the English Delegation to the Reparations Conference in 1932. Mac-Donald and his daughter Ishbel watch Herriot trying to avoid journalists who have waylaid him in the hotel hall after his discussion with the British Prime Minister. Next to MacDonald is his private secretary, Mr. Butler.

At an evening reception at the Disarmament Conference in Geneva, Eduard Beneš (back to camera), the Czechoslovak Foreign Minister, finds himself some attentive listeners. In the first row from left to right: Norman Davis, the American delegate; Edouard Herriot; Joseph Paul-Boncour; Pietri, the Italian delegate; Sir John Simon; Maxim Litvinov, the Soviet Foreign Minister.

The Hungarian statesman and deputy ▶ Count Albert Apponyi during his speech before the Geneva Disarmament Conference in 1932. Behind him from left to right: Czechoslovak Foreign Minister Benes; Politis, the Greek delegate; Sir Eric Drummond, Secretary General of the League of Nations.

Private discussion in Lausanne and Geneva: The picture on top shows Sir Herbert Samuel and Norman Davis listening to Herriot; the picture below shows Count Oberndorff, Foreign Minister von Neurath, and Chancellor Franz von Papen of the German delegation to the Reparations Conference.

Listeners in the assembly hall at Geneva. In the top picture (right), Herriot; in the center picture, the American Norman Davis (left); in the bottom picture, Norman Davis again and, next to him, Hugh Wilson, American envoy in Bern.

The speech of the leader of the German delegation, Rudolf Nadolny, in July, 1932, in which he demanded equal status in armaments for Germany, gave rise to a lively discussion in the French delegation. From left to right: Premier Herriot; State Minister Laurent-Eynac; Pierre Cot, Air Minister; Paul-Boncour, Minister of War. Behind Herriot the French delegate Professor René Cassin. ▶

In front of Ramsay MacDonald's door in the Hotel Beau Rivage in Lausanne, 1932. Left, the hats of the German Chancellor and ▶
his Foreign Minister; right, those of the French delegation.

The Rt. Hon.
J. Ramsay MacDonald

Final session in MacDonald's hotel room in Lausanne, 1932. From left to right: Count Schwerin-Krosigk, German Finance Minister (standing); Jules Renkin, Belgian Premier; Dino Grandi, Italian Foreign Minister; Konstantin von Neurath, German Foreign Minister; Franz von Papen, German Chancellor; Edouard Herriot, French Premier; Duncan Sandys, of the British Embassy in Berlin; Georges Bonnet, French Minister Without Portfolio; Ramsay MacDonald, British Prime Minister; Sir Maurice Hankey, Secretary to the British Cabinet (standing); Germain-Martin (back to camera), French Finance Minister; Emile Francqui, Belgian Finance Minister; and Professor Hesnard, the French interpreter.

CHAPTER FIVE

Judges and Courts

The judiciary is the guardian of the conscience of the people as well as of the law of the land. It has no army or police force to execute its mandates or compel obedience to its decrees. It has no control over the purse strings of government. Those two historic sources of power rest in other hands. The strength of the judiciary is in the command it has over the hearts and minds of men. That respect and prestige are the product of innumerable judgments and decrees, a mosaic built from the multitude of cases decided. Respect and prestige do not grow suddenly; they are the products of time and experience. But they flourish when judges are independent and courageous. The court that raises its hand against the mob may be temporarily unpopular; but it soon wins the confidence of the nation. The court that fails to stand before the mob is not worthy of the great tradition.

—WILLIAM O. DOUGLAS

Johann Hein, a notorious safecracker, stands trial at Coburg on a charge of killing three policemen.

A dramatic moment during the testimony given by Hein's aged mother.

◄ Another famous case, in Berlin-Moabit. Indicted was a gang of criminals who called themselves "Ever-Loyal" *(Immertreu)*. All the counsel for the defense had famous names. From right to left: Dr. Max Alsberg, Dr. Peschke, Dr. Erich Frey (examining a witness), and Feblowicz. Salomon used a tried and true method: he came shortly after the session began and stayed only a short while. Therefore he did not find out until several days later that at the beginning of the trial the President had announced: "Whoever photographs here will get three days in jail."

Germany had not long been a unified nation. Thus, on October 1, 1929, the highest German court—the Reichsgericht in Leipzig—celebrated only its fiftieth anniversary. Salomon—for the occasion—received the first permit to photograph there. From left to right: Government Inspector Machule, Judge Kolb, Judge Veltmann, President of the Senate Dr. Mansfeld, Judge Helber, and Judge Dr. Pinzger.

◀ The High Court in London, 1929: Left, Mr. Justice Avory; right, the Lord Chief Justice, Lord Hewart. In the foreground are the Clerks to the Court. After the death of his friend Avory, Lord Hewart gave permission to publish this photograph, although photographing court proceedings is illegal in England.

Lord Chief Justice Hewart with his wife in their house in Totteridge, near London. Before embarking on his legal career, Hewart had been a well-known journalist.

The Public Prosecutor of the highest Dutch Court (Hooge Raad), L. C. Besier.

The Permanent Court of International Justice at The Hague, Holland, 1932. The center part of the judges' bench. From left to right: Count Rostvorovski, Poland; Guerrero, San Salvador; Baron Mitsudeira Adatci, Japan; Baron Rollin-Jacquemins, Belgium; Henri Fromageot, France; Francisco-José Urruttia, Colombia.

The United States Supreme Court in 1932. From left to right: the Judges Owen J. Roberts, Pierce Butler, Louis D. Brandeis, ▶
Willis Van Devanter, Chief Justice Charles Evans Hughes, George Sutherland, Harlan Fiske Stone, Benjamin N. Cardozo. For
his first attempt to take pictures of the Supreme Court, the editors of *Fortune* gave Salomon the company of four burly reporters,
who were to shield him from the eyes of janitors. But all four left hastily the moment Salomon removed the camera from his coat
pocket. He returned alone the next day with the camera built into an attaché case. To this day there is, presumably, no other
photograph of the Supreme Court in session.

CHAPTER SIX

Artists, Intellectuals, and Society

Paradoxically I have witnessed, in the very period in which our world
has retrogressed morally a thousand years, that same mankind achieve
such unsuspected heights technically and intellectually that it has in one
swoop passed and superseded everything which had been done in a mil-
lion years. Never before has humanity been so satanic in its behavior, so
God-like in its achievements.

—STEFAN ZWEIG

Professor Wilhelm Kahl during a lecture at Berlin University in 1930. Kahl was a university teacher, Reichstag Deputy, Honorary Chairman of the Liberal Union and of the German Peoples' Party, and Chairman of the Committee on Criminal Law in the Reichstag.

Professor Wilhelm His during a lecture on anatomy before students of Berlin University, 1930. ▶

Professor Ferdinand Sauerbruch (at the bed, right) during a refresher course for doctors in Berlin, 1930.

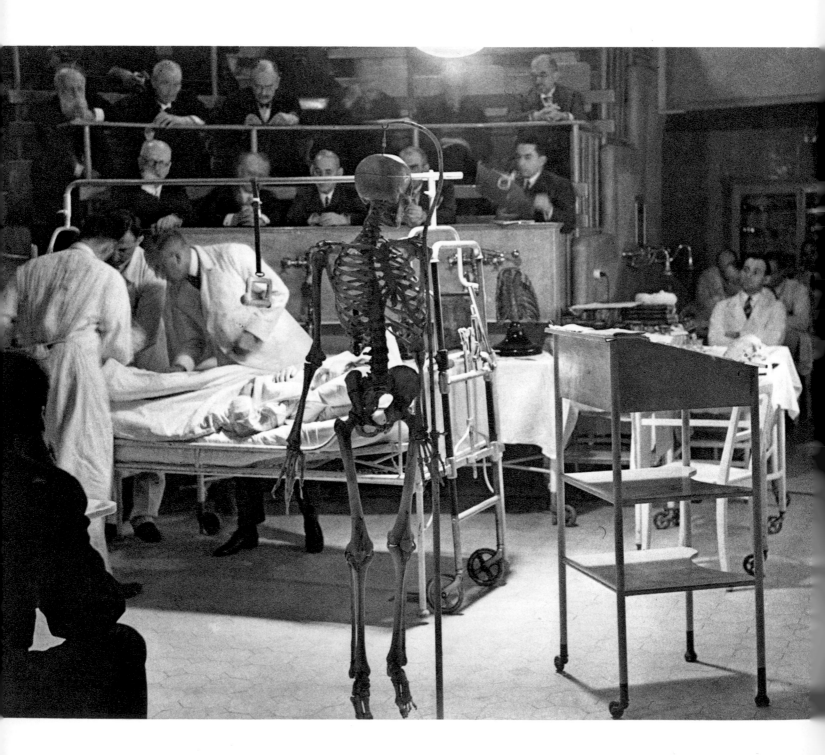

Professor Alfred Adler, the Viennese psychologist, during a guest lecture in the Town Hall of Berlin-Schöneberg, 1930.

Lecture in Brussels in 1935 by Professor Auguste Piccard on his research into the stratosphere. He later turned to research of the ocean depths and, in 1953, made a record descent of 10,335 feet. This work is now being continued by his son Jacques.

The famous Zeppelin skipper Dr. Hugo Eckener, in conversation with Oscar von Miller, founder of the German Museum in Munich, at a dinner given by the American Chamber of Commerce in Berlin.

Meeting of the Poetry Section of the Academy of Arts in Berlin in 1929. From left to right: Alfred Döblin, Thomas Mann, Ricarda Huch, Bernhard Kellermann, Hermann Stehr, and Alfred Mombert. On the opposite page, sitting at the table from left to right: Alfred Mombert, Eduard Stucken, Wilhelm von Scholz, Oskar Loerke, Walter von Molo, President, Ludwig Fulda, Heinrich Mann; standing: Bernhard Kellermann, Alfred Döblin, Thomas Mann, Max Halbe.

Dr. Alfred Kerr, the Berlin theater critic known and feared for his acid reviews.

In 1932, the Goethe Centenary, Gerhart Hauptmann visited New York and gave the major address at Columbia University. Otto H. Kahn, the New York banker, gave a luncheon in his honor. Next to Hauptmann, the wife of the American author Norman Hapgood.

A banquet honoring Gerhart Hauptmann. Eugene Meyer, Governor of the Federal Reserve Board and President of the Reconstruction Finance Corporation, in conversation with Mrs. Margarete Hauptmann.

◄ The Impressionist painter Max Liebermann in his house in Berlin, May, 1931. The painting shows the artist's parents.

Richard Strauss and the opera singer Elisabeth Rethberg at a banquet on the occasion of the premiere of the opera *The Egyptian Helena,* in which Mme. Rethberg sang the leading role. Dresden, 1928.

Bruno Walter conducting. For photographing concerts, Salomon had constructed a tripod that was hardly distinguishable from a music stand. Thus he could sit in the orchestra and take his pictures close up.

Pablo Casals in Munich, 1929. This is the first photograph that was ever made of Casals during a concert. Right: Casals in Paris, 1935.

Wilhelm Furtwängler conducting, The Hague, 1932. After a gala concert in Brussels, not only was Furtwängler presented to Elizabeth, the Queen Mother, but also Salomon. "Oh," she said, turning to the photographer, "I was wondering all through the concert which instrument you played."

126

The Dutch conductor, Willem Mengelberg, with the Amsterdam Concertgebouw Orchestra. Soloist is Yehudi Menuhin, then very young. The picture above shows Menuhin's sister Hephzibah, who often accompanied her brother on the piano.

129

Igor Stravinsky conducting.

Pierre Monteux during a rehearsal.

Arturo Toscanini (right) with Maurice van Praag, manager of the New York Philharmonic Orchestra, in the lobby of the Mayflower Hotel, Washington, 1932.

The first photograph ever made of Toscanini during a concert was taken in 1932 in Baltimore. Soloist was the violinist Adolf Busch.

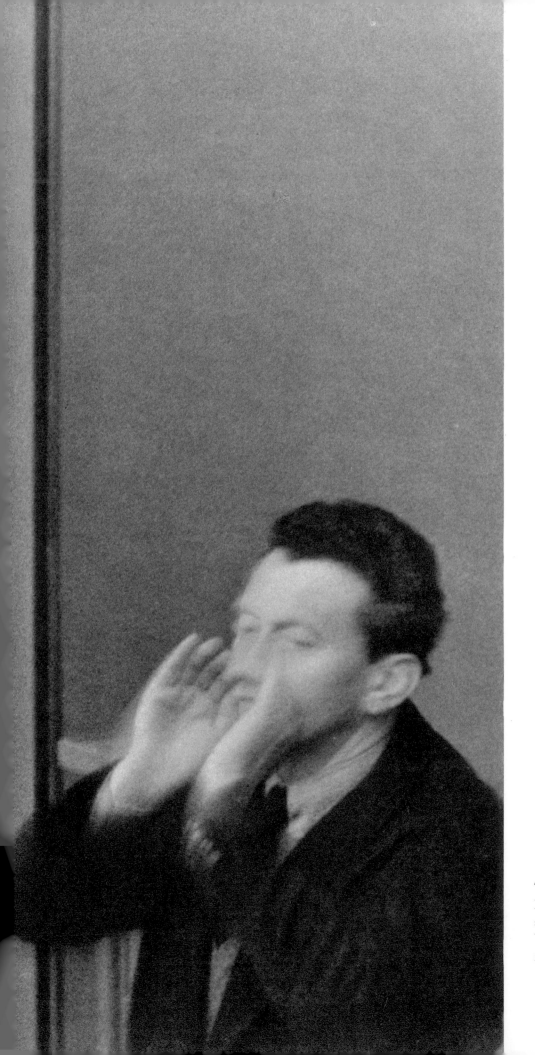

Toscanini during a rehearsal of The Hague Philharmonic Orchestra during a tour of Holland in 1937. Issay Dobrowen, also a conductor, assisted as interpreter.

Sir Thomas Beecham at the conductor's stand of the London Covent Garden Opera, 1936. The only source of light is the reflection of the illuminated music on the stand. Right: One of the boxes at Covent Garden.

At a reception in the Dutch Embassy in London, 1937: Lady Desborough (left) and Miss Eleanor Brougham.

In February, 1935, Dr. Kurt von Schuschnigg, the last Austrian chancellor before the *Anschluss,* visited the British capital. There Baron von Franckenstein, the Austrian envoy, gave a reception in his honor, which closed with a concert. From left to right: Austrian Foreign Minister Baron von Berger-Waldenegg; the Duchess of York, now Queen Mother Elizabeth; Schuschnigg; Princess Helena Victoria; the Duke of York, later King George VI; Prime Minister MacDonald; Hoesch, the German Ambassador.

Elisabeth Schumann sings at a reception of the Austrian Legation in London. From left to right: Dr. Neumayer, the Austrian Finance Minister; the former Spanish Queen, Victoria Eugenia; Baron von Franckenstein, the Austrian envoy; Princess Marina (the Duchess of Kent); Dr. Kienböck, President of the Austrian National Bank; Princess Helena Victoria; Mrs. Campbell.

In the year 1937 another Austrian statesman, Dr. Schmidt, the Foreign Minister, came to London. Before the concert began at the Austrian Legation, Prime Minister Neville Chamberlain chatted with Princess Helena Victoria, the sister of King George V, while Dr. Schmidt spoke to Princess Marie Louise.

On this occasion Richard Tauber, who had recently fled from Nazi Germany, gave a recital. In the first row, from the left: Princess Helena Victoria; Dr. Schmidt; Princess Marie Louise; Lady Augusta Inskip; British Minister of Defense Sir Thomas Inskip, who had come to the concert in his court dress from a reception at Buckingham Palace; and the Duchess of Sutherland.

The picture at top shows Tauber after the concert with his wife, the actress Diana Napier.

◄ Princess Juliana of the Netherlands, who has been Queen of Holland since 1948, at a reception at the Dutch Embassy in London in 1936, shortly before her engagement to Prince Bernhard von Lippe-Biesterfeld. She is seen here conversing with Mr. Volkoff of the Covent Garden Opera and, in the bottom picture, with her lady-in-waiting.

Beniamino Gigli in the Amsterdam Concertgebouw, 1932.

A reception given by Queen Wilhelmina of the Netherlands in the royal palace at The Hague on the occasion of the engage- ▶ ment of her daughter, Juliana, in 1937. This is the first unofficial photograph that the Dutch royal family ever allowed to be taken in the royal palace. Left, next to the Queen, Princess Juliana.

Prominent wedding guests: Premier Dr. H. Colijn (left) and the Ministers van Schaik and van Lidt de Jeude.

A gala concert in the Amsterdam Concertgebouw was part of the celebrations in conjunction with the marriage of Princess Juliana. The wedding pair watched nervously as Queen Wilhelmina's diadem threatened to slip off. The negative of this photograph shows obvious damage. In order to save some of his photographs Salomon cached them in two places in Holland for safekeeping during the war. One part was preserved in the library of the Dutch Parliament; another he buried in the chicken coop of a Dutch friend's house. Over the years, the latter negatives were seriously damaged by dampness.

Princess Juliana and Prince Bernhard during their first joint visit to a session of the Dutch State Council. ▶

View through the church portal shortly after the wedding. In the foreground is F. M. L. Baron van Geen.

Dr. H. Colijn, the Dutch Premier, receives Oswald Pirow at his home. Pirow entertained the ambition of becoming the ▶ "Hitler of South Africa." From the left: Pirow (half from behind); Dr. van Broekhuizen, the South African envoy to The Hague; Dr. Colijn; Dr. Patijn, the Dutch Foreign Minister; and Dr. Hendrik Muller, the former Dutch envoy to Prague. The occasion was Pirow's trip to London and European countries after visiting Hitler at Berchtesgaden.

A meeting of the board of directors of the Royal Dutch Shell company, one of the largest industrial enterprises in the world. Around the table at the company's headquarters at The Hague, 1932, are the directors of the most important of the 500 subsidiary companies comprising the Royal Dutch empire, which may be seen symbolized in a "family tree" on the right of the photograph. From the left: Andrew Agnew, Jonkheer Loudon, Sir Robert Waley-Cohen, G. C. D. Dunlop, August Philips, J. E. F. de Kok, Sir Henri Deterding, J. B. Aug. Kessler, J. Th. Erb, C. J. K. van Aalst, J. Luden, and N. van Wijk. In order to get permission from Sir Henri Deterding to be admitted to this board meeting, Salomon had to take a photograph of the Dutch Cabinet in session and show this to Sir Henri.

CHAPTER SEVEN

America in 1930

For our New World I consider far less important for what it has done, or what it is, than for results to come. Sole among nationalities, these States have assumed the task to put in forms of lasting power and practicality, on areas of amplitude rivaling the operations of the physical kosmos, the moral speculations of ages, long, long deferred, the democratic republican principle, and the theory of development and perfection by voluntary standards, and self-reliance. Who else, indeed, except the United States, in history, so far, have accepted in unwitting faith, and, as we now see, stand, act upon, and go securely for, these things?

—WALT WHITMAN

◀ In the lobby of the St. Francis Hotel in San Francisco, 1929. Concerned stockholders follow the movements of the stock exchange.

William Randolph Hearst with his guests at a luncheon on his ranch, La Cuesta Encantada, San Simeon, California, 1930. In the foreground (in polka-dotted dress), Miss Marion Davies. Hearst's ranch, stuffed with art treasures imported from Europe, was built in the style of a Spanish cathedral of the sixteenth century. Special trains brought Hearst's guests directly from Hollywood to the property, where they alighted at a private railroad station.

160

A few years later Hearst purchased a further property in Britain, St. Donat's Castle in Wales. Among the guests who attended a dinner party there in 1935 were, from left to right, Mrs. Jack Mulhall, wife of the American film actor; Randolph Churchill, son of Winston Churchill; Miss Marion Davies; and Sir Charles Allom, the architect who had remodeled St. Donat's Castle for Hearst.

In San Simeon, Hearst was accustomed to retire after meals in order to study reports from his dozens of newspapers. To maintain contact with the outside world, Hearst had established at his ranch his own post office.

◀ James Hamilton Lewis, Senator from Illinois, during a meeting of the Senate Foreign Affairs Committee in 1932.

Senators Couzens, Robinson, and Schall (from left to right) of the Senate Judiciary Committee during a Washington meeting in February, 1932.

Foreign diplomats in the waiting room of Henry L. Stimson, Secretary of State, in the Department of State, Washington, 1932. On the sofa from left: Paul Claudel, the French poet and ambassador in Washington; the Swiss envoy, Peter; and the German ambassador, Dr. Fr. W. von Prittwitz und Gaffron. Respectfully seated on a chair nearby: Micheli, First Secretary of the Swiss Legation.

After his visit to Berlin in 1931, Pierre Laval, then French premier, came to the United States. This photograph was taken during ▶ an evening reception in Senator Borah's home. Borah (in the middle) was Chairman of the Senate Foreign Affairs Committee. To the right, half hidden, is Laval; to the left, Harrison, Vice-President of the Federal Reserve Board.

An historic moment in October, 1931, in the White House in Washington. Laval persuaded President Herbert Hoover to permit Salomon to be the first photographer to take informal photographs in the White House. Hoover did not speak French, nor Laval, English; therefore the first shot (above) shows what appear to be stiff posed smiles. On the enlarged picture (right), behind Laval and to the left is Boissard, French Ministerial Director; next to Hoover (standing), Ogden Mills, Undersecretary of State, and Secretary of State Henry L. Stimson.

President Herbert Hoover as guest of honor at the annual dinner of the White House Correspondents' Association, March, 1932. The camera was less than three feet away, hidden in a flowerpot and triggered by a remote-control cable.

Alfred E. Smith, former Governor of New York and the only Catholic candidate for the presidency prior to John F. Kennedy, at a Jackson Day Dinner in Washington, 1932.

172

In June, 1932, Max Schmeling was scheduled to fight Jack Sharkey for the World Heavyweight Championship. Franklin Delano Roosevelt, then Governor of New York, came to the training camp in Kingston, New York. The picture shows Mrs. Eleanor Roosevelt and the Governor in conversation with the German Consul, Mr. Schwarz.

After the training session the future President greeted Schmeling. ▶

A view of Jauntig's Bar, New York, 1932.

From a series of pictures taken on Ellis Island, where illegal immigrants to the U.S. were detained. Not until the 1950's was this famous station closed. Below, inmates write home. Right, a little family.

A Hollywood party in 1930. From left to right: the German Consul in San Francisco, Dr. von Hentig; Dolores del Rio; Ernst Lubitsch; Maurice Chevalier; Madame Chevalier; Vilma Banky; Paul Kohner, a film producer; Carl Laemmle.

Dolores del Rio and John Farrow at the same party. ▶

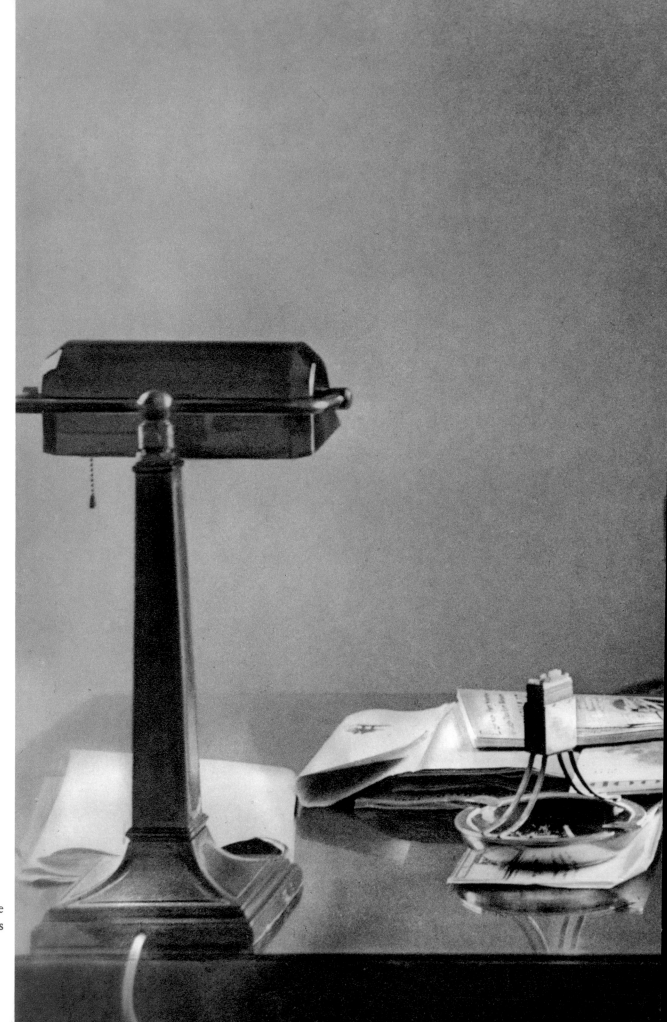

Ernst Lubitsch, the director, in his Hollywood office.

Shortly after the installation of the first transatlantic telephone cable, Marlene Dietrich spoke to her little daughter in Berlin from her Hollywood home. The long-distance call actually took place at 4.00 A.M., but the film star was persuaded to repeat the experience for Salomon's camera.

In the course of a tour of Europe on which Salomon accompanied the conductor Furtwängler, he discovered that Charlie Chaplin was on the same Channel steamer. Salomon decided to ask them to pose together for a picture. While Salomon was putting his case to Chaplin's secretary, Chaplin declared that he had never heard of Furtwängler, and besides he was already in bed. Salomon finally succeeded in getting his picture the next morning at 6:30 A.M., just before the ship anchored. The two men (picture left) shook hands in silence, looked courteously at the camera, and then separated without a word.

In 1930 Eisenstein, the Russian director, came to Hollywood on his way to Mexico, where he was to shoot a film that he ▶ never finished. The photograph shows him (left) with his host, the author Upton Sinclair, on the Sinclairs' tennis court.

In Washington, 1932, Dr. Benvenuto Hauptmann, the son of the poet Gerhart Hauptmann, in conversation with Miss Mary White.

Otto H. Kahn, the banker, and his wife
in their New York mansion.

CHAPTER EIGHT

A Look at France in 1935

France's *raison d'être* is to annoy and inconvenience the world. She was created to that end, and has become a gadfly attacking whatever personalities are entrenched in power, whatever systems call themselves eternal. These attacks are just wherever justice is perverted. . . . It is a healthy human mind which seeks to expose injustice and atone for it. As long as there is a France worthy of the name, its influence will spread in the world, and those nations which have risen high will have no rest whether they have earned their place through work, power, or bluster. There is something in order, calm and opulence that slaps mankind and freedom in the face. To smoke this thing out and expose it is the duty of France.

—JEAN GIRAUDOUX

◄ Maurice Privat, Pierre Laval's astrologer, seated under Rubens' huge painting "The Conclusion of Peace," in the Quai d'Orsay, awaiting the daily conference with his master. Paris, 1935.

Laval delivers a speech from his seat in the Chamber of Deputies. Next to him, Edouard Herriot.

On this day the spectators' gallery of the French Chamber is filled to ▶ overflowing. Many of the female listeners are the wives of the deputies debating bitterly in the Hall below.

A small debate, and a large one, in the Chamber of Deputies.

A visit to General Braconnier, Chief of the Military Cabinet, in the Elysée Palace, seat of the French President. The General at his desk and in the bosom of his family, 1937.

Madame Philippe Berthelot, wife of the Secretary General of the Quai d'Orsay, with friends at home, 1932.

After the Press Conference: Jules Sauerwein (left), diplomatic correspondent of *Le Matin* and later of *Paris-Soir*, enjoys a discussion with Mr. Polak of the Agence Economique.

CHAPTER NINE

On the Eve of World War II

Nor can the United States escape the censure of history. Absorbed in their own affairs and all the abounding interest, activities, and accidents of a free community, they simply gaped at the vast changes which were taking place in Europe, and imagined they were no concern of theirs. . . . If the influence of the United States had been exerted, it might have galvanised the French and British politicians into action. The League of Nations, battered though it had been, was still an august instrument which would have invested any challenge to the new Hitler war-menace with the sanctions of international law. Under the strain the Americans merely shrugged their shoulders, so that in a few years they had to pour out the blood and treasures of the New World to save themselves from mortal danger.

—WINSTON S. CHURCHILL

During a conference at the Palace Hotel, Montreux, in July, 1936, ex-King Alfonso XIII of Spain managed to corner Pierre Laval for an instant. The last picture bears witness to the doubtful outcome of the conversation.

Haile Selassie, Emperor of Abyssinia, at one of the formal dinners in his honor held during his exile in London, 1936. Left, Sir Archibald Sinclair, the Secretary of State for Air; right, Sir A. Paige, the historian.

View of the assembly hall of the League of Nations, Geneva, during the Debate on Abyssinia in July, 1936. Practically only ▶ Abyssinian delegates are present in the room listening to their countrymen argue against Italian aggression.

Before his departure from Geneva, the Abyssinian Emperor took a last look back at the Palace of the League of Nations.

◄ Detectives and the bodyguards of diplomats during the Montreux Conference in 1936.

A garden party given by the Secretary General of the League of Nations, Joseph Avenol, in Geneva in 1936. From left to right: Avenol's Cabinet Chief Hodén; French Premier Léon Blum; Soviet Foreign Minister Maxim Litvinov.

In July, 1936, the plenary meeting of the League of Nations got a glimpse of Nazi manners with Senate President Greiser of Danzig. After Greiser gave two tirades he left his seat, and passing the press gallery, he cocked a snook and stuck out his tongue at the journalists sitting there.

In effect, this incident ended League of Nations control over the city of Danzig. In the picture at the left, Colonel Joseph Beck, Poland's Foreign Minister, is talking over the affair with Anthony Eden. In the photograph on the right, Sean Lester, High Commissioner of Danzig, talks to Beck, reclining on the sofa.

◄ In November, 1937, a Nine-Power Conference on problems in the Far East took place in Brussels. From left to right: Yvon Delbos, the French Foreign Minister; Paul Henri Spaak, the Belgian Foreign Minister; Anthony Eden, the British Foreign Secretary.

Dinner party at the Austrian Legation in London in 1937 on the occasion of the coronation of King George VI: Winston Churchill between Lady Maud Hoare (left), wife of Sir Samuel Hoare, and Mrs. Cochrane Baillie.

Two additional photographs of the same party in the Austrian Legation. From left to right: the host, Baron von Franckenstein; ▶ Lord Bessborough, former Governor General of Canada; Churchill; the Austrian Foreign Minister, Dr. Schmidt.

214

Publisher's Note

The pictures used in this volume came from those of Erich Salomon's prints and negatives which have remained in good condition to this day. Even before the Nazis confiscated his apartment in The Hague in 1943, Salomon was sufficiently farsighted to have hidden one group of negatives under the chicken coop of a friend's house and to have given another set to the library of the Dutch Parliament for safekeeping. A third section of his archives survived the war in England in the care of Peter Hunter, who in 1952 brought together all this material in Amsterdam. Magnum of New York prepared a second collection in New York City.

Technical notes: Salomon first worked with the Ernemann Ermanox *f.*2 camera; from 1932 on he used a Leica more and more frequently and took most of his photographs with that camera.

For the Ermanox he utilized glass plates, 4.5 by 6 cm. in size in individual cassettes. He was known to carry thirty of these at one time in his trouser pocket; and he held a ready reserve in the outside pockets of his jacket. The system worked especially well when someone wanted to confiscate his photographs; he would invariably give up slides from the "unexposed" pocket.

Salomon took time exposures when making interior shots. He would vary the exposure time according to the movements made by the people he was trying to photograph. He was extraordinarily clever in catching the most favorable psychological moment. When, for instance, a speaker's hand stood still for just a quarter of a second in the midst of an expressive gesture, this would suffice for a proper exposure. The material for negatives became more and more sensitive to light from 1931 on, though the maximum sensitivity available even in 1940 cannot be compared with that of today's films. With the exception of longer developing time and occasionally intensifying underexposed negatives, Salomon used only the techniques common to his contemporaries. He developed all his own negatives— often in hotel rooms and once in a while in the sleeper of a Pullman car. At times he employed an assistant to help with the printing.

Some of the photographs in this book were displayed at the following exhibitions of Erich Salomon's work:

1935 London, Royal Photographic Society
1937 London, Ilford Galleries
1956 Cologne, *Photokina*
1956 Berlin, Town Hall Berlin-Schöneberg
1957 Hamburg, *Museum für Kunst und Gewerbe* (Museum of Arts and Crafts)
1957 London, Royal Photographic Society
1957 Leiden, University *(Prentenkabinet)*
1957 Stuttgart, *Landesgewerbemuseum* (Provincial Crafts Museum)
1958 Rochester, N. Y., George Eastman House
1958 New York, Time & Life Building
1958 Washington, D. C., Library of Congress; followed by exhibitions in twelve
        American cities, arranged by the Smithsonian Institution
1963 Cologne, *Photokina,* as part of an exhibition entitled *Great Photographers of this Century*

Most of the exhibitions that took place after 1956 were due to the efforts of Fritz Gruber. Gruber became interested in Erich Salomon's work as long ago as January, 1930, when Gruber was a twenty-one-year-old journalist. His admiration for Salomon reawakened when he was arranging the 1956 *Photokina* exhibition in Cologne. His contribution to photography and to the work of Erich Salomon is mentioned here in appreciation. The editors also wish to thank the many others who stood by them with help and advice. They are too numerous to list by name.

Selected Bibliography

CRAIG, GORDON A., and FELIX GILBERT (Editors). *The Diplomats: 1919–1939.* Princeton, N. J., Princeton University Press, 1953.

GATHORNE-HARDY, G. M. *A Short History of International Affairs, 1920–1939.* London, Oxford University Press, 1950.

GERNSHEIM, HELMUT. *Creative Photography.* London, Faber and Faber, 1962.

—— and GERNSHEIM, ALISON. *The History of Photography.* London, Oxford University Press, 1955.

HICKS, WILSON. *Words and Pictures: An Introduction to Photo-Journalism.* New York, Harper & Row, 1952.

JUDGE, JACQUELYN. *Available Light* (ed. George Wright). New York, American Photographic Book Publishing Co., 1955.

NEWHALL, BEAUMONT. *The History of Photography, 1839–1965.* Garden City, N. Y., Doubleday, 1965.

—— and NEWHALL, NANCY. *Masters of Photography.* New York, George Braziller, Inc. 1958.

POLLACK, PETER. *The Picture History of Photography.* New York, Harry N. Abrams, Inc., 1958.

SALOMON, ERICH. *Berühmte Zeitgenossen in Unbewachten Augenblicken.* Stuttgart, J. Engelhorns Nachfolger, 1931.

Index of Names

The figures at the right refer to the page on which the caption appears.

221